# Coming to America

## The Story of Immigration

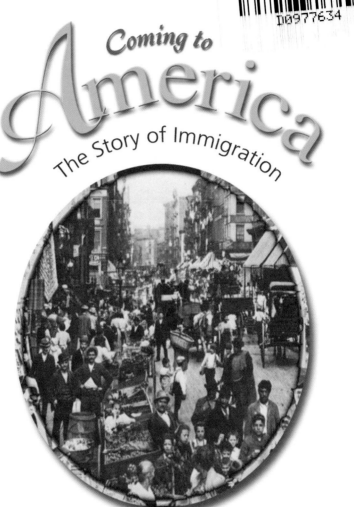

Joanne Mattern

Perfection Learning®

# Dedication

For my grandmother, who made the long journey to America

# About the Author

Joanne Mattern is the author of many books for children. Her favorite topics include animals, biography, and history. She especially likes writing nonfiction because it allows her to bring real people, places, and events to life. "I firmly believe that everything in the world is a story waiting to be told."

Along with writing, Joanne enjoys speaking to school and community groups about the topics in her books. She is also a huge baseball fan and enjoys music and needlework.

Joanne lives in the Hudson Valley of New York State with her husband and young daughter. The family also includes a greyhound and two cats, and "more animals are always welcome."

**Inside Illustration:** Margaret Sanfilippo
**Cover and Book Design:** Deborah Lea Bell

**Image Credits:** ArtToday (some images copyright www.arttoday.com) Dover Publications pp. 6, 41 **Dynamic Graphics** p. 27 **Library of Congress** pp. 22, 31, 36, 40, 47, 48, 56, 57, 59 **National Park Service** pp. 30, 38

# Table of Contents

# Leaving Home

Lena Martini was excited. She was scared too. Today, she would leave her home and start the long journey to America.

Twelve-year-old Lena had lived her whole life on a farm in northern Italy. She helped her mother in the house. She cooked and cleaned. She also took care of her four-year-old sister, Mary. Lena's big brother, Nick, worked on the farm.

For the past few years, life on the farm had been hard. The Martinis only worked on the farm. They did not own the land. They had to give most of the food they raised to the man who owned the farm. There was little left to feed themselves.

Nick was 16. He was old enough to work in the town 20 miles away. But so many people were looking for jobs. Nick could not find work there.

When Lena was ten years old, Uncle Mario and Papa sat down in the kitchen of their little house. She listened as they talked.

"I hear there are many jobs in America," Uncle Mario said. "Our cousin Frank told me that Americans are very rich. Their streets are even paved with gold. You can get anything you want there. Why don't we go to America?"

Papa nodded. "We could have a better life there," he agreed.

"But where will we get the money for our tickets?" Mama asked.

"Mario and I have been thinking about going to America for a long time," Papa said. "We have saved some money. There is enough for the two of us to go. When we get there, we will find jobs. We will send you money. Then you and the children can join us there."

So Lena's father and uncle left the farm and went to America. Lena missed them very much.

Many months passed before they heard from Papa and Uncle Mario. Finally, a letter came. It said that they had rented an apartment. It was in a big city called New York.

They had found jobs too. Both of them worked laying bricks for a new building.

"The streets are not paved with gold here after all," Papa wrote. "But there is plenty of work in this big city."

"The streets are not paved with gold here after all," Papa wrote. "But there is plenty of work in this big city. We will send money for your tickets as soon as we can."

It took two years before Papa and Uncle Mario had enough money for the rest of the family to join them.

At last, another letter came. Folded inside a piece of paper was $100. Lena had never seen so much money. It was enough to buy four tickets to America. There was even some money left.

Mama sent Nick to town to buy tickets from the **steamship** office. Nick also arranged for a horse and wagon to come to their house. It would take the family and their things to Genoa.

Genoa was a busy **seaport**. There the family would board a ship called the *Barbarossa*. That ship would take them to America.

The family had a lot to do before they left. Lena's

mother sold all of their furniture. She also
sold most of the family's dishes and
other things. It would be too hard
to take everything.

Mama did keep a beautiful
china plate that had belonged to
her grandmother. That plate was
carefully packed between layers of
clothing in a trunk.

"We can't carry very much with us,"
Mama told the children. "You can each choose one thing
to take."

Mary chose her rag doll. Lena kept a book she had
gotten at school. Nick picked a set of tools his father had
left for him. Mama picked the family Bible. Everything
was carefully packed into the trunk. The family was ready
to begin their long journey to America.

# Why Did People Come to America?

Over 20 million people left their homes in Europe. They came to America between 1892 and 1924. Most of them had no jobs waiting for them. They brought little money and few possessions. They knew that once they arrived, they would probably never again see their **homeland** or the people they left behind.

What would make people leave everything? What would make them travel far across an ocean? What would make them start a new life in a strange country?

People left for four basic reasons.
- **Famine**
- Wars and unrest
- Religious **persecution**
- Desire for a better future

# Famine

In the 1800s, many Europeans made a living by farming. If bad weather or disease destroyed the crops, there was nothing to eat.

One of the most famous famines happened in Ireland during the 1840s. Irish **peasants** depended entirely on potatoes for their food. In 1845, a disease destroyed the entire potato crop.

Nearly two million people died of starvation or disease. The survivors knew their future depended on one thing. They had to leave Ireland. They had to go where there was plenty of food. They headed for America.

People in other countries also left home. During the 1860s, famine struck Sweden. Whole villages packed up and came to America.

## Wars and Unrest

During the 1800s and early 1900s, Europe was a place of violent change. Many countries were torn apart by war. Millions of people became **refugees**. They left their homes to escape danger and unfair treatment.

In 1848, a group of Germans tried to change their country's government. They were called the "Forty-Eighters." They did not succeed. Many chose to leave Germany. That was better than being arrested by the government.

Many people left Europe to avoid serving in the armies. Many times, **ethnic groups** were forced into an army of another country. They were treated badly. For example, the Turks had killed millions of Armenian families. But Armenians were forced to serve in Turkey's armies.

After World War II (1939–1945), many countries in Europe came under the rule of the **Communist** party. This government limited people's freedom. Many did not want to live under those conditions. During the 1950s, the United States (U.S.) passed special laws called **Refugee Acts**. These acts admitted over 250,000 Eastern Europeans to the U.S.

## Religious Persecution

People want to be free to practice their religion. This desire for religious freedom has always been an important reason for **immigration**. The Puritans landed at Plymouth Rock in 1620. They came in order to practice their religion freely. Other examples include the large numbers of Quakers who left Norway in 1825.

Throughout history, Jews have been persecuted for their faith. In the late 1800s and early 1900s, thousands of Russian Jews were killed in **pogroms**. These were mass killings organized by the government or by churches. More than two million Jews left Russia and eastern Europe. In the years before

12

World War II, many Jews fled persecution by the Nazis in Germany, Austria, and other European countries.

## The Desire for a Better Future

Perhaps the biggest reason people came to America was the desire for a better future. During the late 19th and early 20th centuries, many people believed that America was a "Golden Land." It was a place where anyone could get a decent job, go to a free school, and have plenty to eat.

It was a common belief that the streets were paved with gold. Children were told that candy would fall right from the sky into their mouths.

In Europe, many people found it hard to find jobs or earn enough money to survive. **Industrialization** meant that machines replaced workers in cities and towns. New machinery also put many small farmers out of work. At the same time, industrial growth in America created jobs.

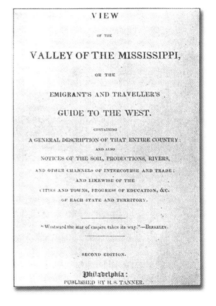

Many immigrants were drawn to America because of cheap, plentiful land. In the 1860s, the U.S. government passed a law called the **Homestead Act**. This law allowed anyone to claim 160 acres of land in the western U.S. All an individual had to do was live on the land for five years. Then it would belong to that person.

Some western states advertised their growing towns and cheap farmland in European newspapers. Often the ads were not true. But people came anyway, searching for a better life.

# Boarding the Ship

On April 8, 1906, a horse-drawn wagon pulled up in front of the Martinis' house. It was early in the morning. Nick carried out the trunk holding the family's belongings. He placed it in the wagon with the other bundles. Then he helped Mama, Lena, and Mary climb on.

"*Addio*!" Nick called to their little house. Then he jumped into the wagon. "Good-bye!"

It took two days for the wagon to get to Genoa. Lena soon got tired of the bumpy ride. "Mama, it feels like my teeth are going to fall right out of my mouth," she complained. "And all this bumping is hurting my legs."

Sometimes Mama let the children get out of the wagon and walk alongside. But that wasn't very comfortable either. The road was made of dirt and rough stones. Lena's shoes were thin. And the rocks hurt her feet. Soon she climbed back into the wagon.

"I'm glad we don't have to take a wagon all the way to America," Mary said.

Finally, the Martinis arrived in Genoa. Lena couldn't believe her eyes. She held tightly to her mother's and sister's hands.

Lena looked around. She had never seen so many people and buildings crowded together.

"Papa says that New York City is even bigger and more crowded," Nick whispered.

"Stay close together!" Mama ordered. "I don't want anyone to get lost."

The family made its way to the steamship office. Lena clutched Mary's hand even tighter.

The steamship office was jammed with people. The family waited in a long line. Finally they were able to talk to a man behind a window. Nick showed the man their tickets.

"Your ship is the *Barbarossa*," the man said. "It leaves on Thursday. That's three days from now." He gave Nick a piece of paper. "Here is a hotel where you can stay until it's time to leave."

The hotel was filled with many other families going to America. Lena made friends with a girl named Theresa. Her family was also sailing to New York City on the *Barbarossa*. The two girls played together in the hotel rooms. Their mothers would not let them go outside. They were afraid the girls might get lost in the busy streets.

Early Thursday morning, Lena, Theresa, and their families went back to the steamship office. They still had a lot to do before they could get on the ship.

First, a doctor looked at everyone. He had to make sure the passengers were healthy. Anyone who was sick could not get on the boat. Lena saw a young woman taken aside by the doctor. The woman had a bad cough.

"She might have **tuberculosis**," Lena's mother told her. "They won't let her into America if she is sick."

Fortunately, everyone in Lena's family was healthy. But they still had more inspections to go through. First the men and women were separated into two groups. Lena and Mary followed their mother into a room. They had to scrub themselves with nasty-smelling soap. Then a woman combed everyone's hair.

"She's looking for bugs," Lena's mother told her. Lena shuddered. She didn't have any bugs in her hair!

"She's looking for bugs," Lena's mother told her. Lena shuddered. She didn't have any bugs in her hair!

After they finished getting washed and inspected, Lena saw her brother waiting for them. She hardly recognized Nick. His long, thick hair had been cut close

## Long Hair and Lice

All people took an **antiseptic** bath before they were allowed to board the ship. And they had their hair inspected. Many men and boys even had their hair cut short.

These steps were taken to prevent the spread of **lice**. These tiny insects lived in people's hair and carried serious diseases.

Living conditions at this time were crowded and dirty. People weren't able to keep as clean as they do today.

The shipping companies wanted to prevent the spread of disease. They also knew that the sick would not be allowed to enter the U.S. If people were turned away, they were returned to their homeland at the expense of the shipping company.

to his head! Lena saw that all the other men now had short hair too.

"Can we get on the ship now?" Lena asked her mother. But there was still one more thing to do.

A man came over to Mama. He asked her questions about the family. He wanted to know their names, how old they were, and where they were going in America. The man wrote all the information down on a piece of paper. Then he gave each of the Martinis a tag with a number.

"You must show this when you get to New York," he said. Finally, the family was allowed to board the ship.

The Martinis boarded the ship. They were led down several flights of stairs. Finally, they reached the bottom of the ship. This area was called **steerage**. It was where all the families would live during the journey.

"Men to the right. Women and children to the left," one of the sailors told them. Nick waved and followed the other men and

older boys into a separate room.

Lena and Mary stayed with their mother. They made their way into the women's quarters.

Lena saw rows of bunk beds lining a long, narrow room. Her mother quickly claimed two beds.

"I'll take the top bed," she said. "Lena and Mary, you can share the bottom."

Lena sat down on the narrow bed. It didn't even have a mattress, just a blanket and a small, hard pillow. The air was hot and stuffy. And the room was so noisy! Crying babies and shouting adults filled the air with a wall of sound.

"How can we ever sleep with so much noise?" Lena wondered aloud.

"Mama, I have to go to the bathroom," Mary whined.

"Where is the bathroom?" Mama asked.

"It is at the end of the ship," said a woman next to them. She pointed down the long room.

"How can we ever sleep with so much noise?" Lena wondered aloud.

19

"We all have to share one bathing area," the woman added.

Lena's mother sighed as she carried Mary through the crowds of people.

Mary and Mama returned from the bathroom. A screech from the ship's whistle pierced the air. Everyone rushed upstairs to the deck.

"We must be leaving Genoa," Mama said. "Let's go up and watch."

The Martinis joined the crowd moving up the steps. Lena felt the ship sway and rock under her feet. The boat pulled away from the dock and into the waters of the Mediterranean Sea. Lena saw the buildings of Genoa grow smaller and smaller.

Everyone was shouting and crying. Lena felt her mother's arm squeeze tight around her shoulders. She looked up and saw tears running down Mama's face. "*Addio, Italia,*" she said. "Good-bye, Italy."

Lena wondered if any of them would ever see their homeland again.

# On the Ocean

The trip to America took two weeks. Lena soon grew used to the rocking ship. But Mama was not so lucky. She was very **seasick** and could hardly eat. She spent most of the trip lying in her bed. She tried not to vomit.

Many other passengers were also seasick. It didn't take long before the living quarters smelled worse than ever.

Lena, her brother, and her sister spent as much time as they could on the deck of the ship. The fresh, salty air felt good after the stuffy steerage quarters.

Nick made friends with Enrico, one of the sailors. He spent a lot of time helping Enrico do his chores.

Lena played with her friend, Theresa, and kept an eye on little Mary. The girls loved to run up and down the deck and look out at the endless ocean around them.

At night, everyone gathered in steerage. They told stories and sang songs. One man brought a violin and played lively songs so people could dance. Women sewed and talked to one another.

Lena didn't like the cramped steerage

quarters. But she disliked the ship's food even more. Twice a day, the immigrants were given soup and boiled potatoes. Sometimes they had a piece of stringy beef or dried fish.

Lena thought of the fresh fruits and vegetables they ate on the farm at home. She wondered if they had fruits and vegetables in America.

One night, there was a terrible storm. Lena and Mary huddled on their bunk. The ship rocked and tossed in the waves. Lena could hear the howling wind and the pounding rain.

Many of the steerage passengers screamed and cried. Others got sick. Lena's mother prayed in a loud voice. "Don't let us die!" she screamed.

In the morning, the ocean was calm again. Lena was glad to go up on the deck. She breathed the fresh, clean air. She hoped there would be no more storms before the *Barbarossa* reached America.

## Dangers and Disasters

Storms, shipwrecks, fires, and disease were always a threat to ships. A bad storm could sink a ship. It could even wash passengers and crew overboard. Storms could also add days, or even weeks, to the journey.

Ships could also be damaged when they ran onto rocks near shore, struck icebergs, or even hit other ships. Perhaps the most tragic shipwreck was the loss of the British ship *Titanic*. The *Titanic* hit an iceberg on April 14, 1912. When it sank in the North Atlantic, 825 passengers and 673 crew members drowned. Seventy-five percent of the steerage passengers, mostly immigrants, died.

Ship fires also claimed many lives. The worst fire disaster in Atlantic shipping history was the loss of the steamship *Austria*. Crew members were **fumigating**, or cleaning, the steerage compartment with hot tar. Some of the tar spilled on deck and set it on fire. Only 67 of the 567 immigrants on board survived the disaster.

Perhaps the biggest danger to immigrants was disease. In the mid-1800s, ship conditions were so crowded and dirty that diseases spread rapidly. Many people died of **typhus** and **cholera**. Some newspapers called the ships *floating coffins*.

Conditions improved during the 1880s. By then, most immigrants traveled by steamships. These ships were

larger and made of iron or steel. By using iron or steel instead of wood, the risk of fire was less.

These ships could also withstand storms and rough seas better than wooden ships could. And steamships were fast. They could cross the Atlantic in just 8 to 14 days. Earlier ships took about 40 days to make the trip.

Finally, steamships had a doctor on board. Sick passengers could be separated from other passengers and treated. These improvements led to healthier immigrants and dramatically cut the loss of life on ships.

# Ellis Island

Two weeks after they boarded the *Barbarossa*, Lena and her family heard the words they had been waiting for. "Land ho!" a sailor cried from the front of the ship. "Land ho!"

Lena, Mary, and Theresa ran to the railing for a look. Lena's mother, who had finally gotten over her seasickness, followed them.

Lena leaned over the railing and squinted. Sure enough, she could make out a dark shadow along the water. It still looked far away. But it was land!

Nick hurried over to join them. "Enrico told me we will sail into New York Harbor. The ship will take us to a place called **Ellis Island.**"

"What is Ellis Island?" Lena asked. "Is it part of New York City?"

"No. But it is near New York City. Ellis Island is a government immigration station. Enrico says we all have to go there. We will have to answer some questions. Then we'll be allowed to go into America."

"Will Papa be there?" Mary asked.

*Ellis Island*

"I hope so," Mama said. "Now let's go downstairs and get dressed. We want to look nice to go into America."

Most of the immigrants had the same idea. The steerage

26

was crowded with happy people. They were all putting on their best clothes and fixing their hair. Lena smiled as her mother pulled her hair back with a huge bow. Their journey was almost over!

Soon she was dressed. Lena hurried back up on deck.

"Look!" someone shouted. "There is New York City!"

Lena looked in amazement at the buildings crowding the shoreline. This city made Genoa look small! And she had

never seen so many ships in one place! The harbor was jammed with steamships like the *Barbarossa*. Each one was full of immigrants leaning over the railings to get their first look at their new home.

"Who is that lady?" Mary asked.

"Who is that lady?"

Mary asked.

Lena's little sister was pointing at a huge statue in the harbor. The statue was of a woman holding a torch. She seemed to watch as the ship, full of immigrants, sailed below her.

"That is the Statue of Liberty," a man said. He was standing next to the girls. "She was a gift to the U.S. from France back in 1886."

# Statue of Liberty Statistics

Auguste Bartholdi was a French sculptor. He designed the Statue of Liberty and helped raise funds to build it. The French donated about $250,000 for the statue, and the Americans gave about $280,000 for the pedestal.

The French presented the statue to the Minister of the United States in Paris on July 4, 1884. It was shipped to the United States in 214 cases in 1885. It was assembled on Bedloe's Island (now called Liberty Island), overlooking New York Harbor. President Grover Cleveland dedicated the monument on October 28, 1886.

| | | |
|---|---|---|
| Height from base to torch | 151' 1" | 46.50 m |
| Ground to tip of torch | 305' 1" | 92.99 m |
| Heel to top of head | 111' 1" | 33.86 m |
| Length of hand | 16' 5" | 5.00 m |
| Index finger | 8' 0" | 2.44 m |
| Head from chin to cranium | 17' 3" | 5.26 m |
| Head thickness ear to ear | 10' 0" | 3.05 m |
| Distance across each eye | 2' 6" | .76 m |
| Length of nose | 4' 6" | 1.48 m |
| Length of right arm | 42' 0" | 12.80 m |
| Thickness of right arm | 12' 0" | 3.66 m |
| Thickness of waist | 35' 0" | 10.67 m |
| Width of mouth | 3' 0" | .91 m |
| Length of tablet | 23' 7" | 7.19 m |
| Width of tablet | 13' 7" | 4.14 m |
| Thickness of tablet | 2' 0" | .61 m |
| Ground to top of pedestal | 154' 0" | 46.71 m |

354 steps to the crown
192 steps to reach the top of the pedestal
25 windows in the crown (symbolize 25 gemstones found on earth)
7 rays (representing the seven seas and continents of the world)
Tablet says in Roman numerals July 4, 1776
Total weight of copper in the statue is 62,000 lbs (31 tons)
Total weight of steel in the statue is 250,000 lbs (125 tons)
Total weight of the concrete foundation is 54 million lbs (27,000 tons)
Winds of 50 mph cause a statue sway of 3" (7.62cm)
Winds of 50 mph cause a torch sway of 5" (12.70cm)

"It looks like she is welcoming us to America," Lena said.

"And there is Ellis Island," the man continued. He pointed to the brick and stone buildings on a nearby island. "That will be our first stop in America."

Lena expected the *Barbarossa* to pull right up to Ellis Island. Instead, a small **ferry** sailed alongside the bigger ship. Nick helped his mother and sisters into a long line of immigrants waiting to get on the ferry.

"Enrico says the waters around Ellis Island are too shallow for a big ship like the *Barbarossa*," Nick explained. "That's why we have to take a smaller ship to get there."

They got off the ferry on Ellis Island. The Martinis stood in another long line. Along with their shipmates, they inched their way into the main building. Nick dragged the family's trunk behind him.

"You can leave your baggage here," a worker called as the immigrants walked into the building. Behind him, Lena saw a room filled with boxes, baskets, trunks, and bundles. But Nick shook his head. He held on to the trunk.

"Remember the letter Papa sent?" Nick said. "He said some people had their baggage stolen here. I'm not letting this trunk out of my sight."

Lena looked ahead. The line of immigrants made its way up a steep flight of stairs. Lena noticed several men standing at the top of the stairs. These men watched the immigrants as they walked. "Who are they?" she asked her big brother.

"They're doctors," Nick told her. "They are looking for people who have trouble climbing the stairs. Those people might be sick."

When the Martinis reached the top of the stairs, two doctors were waiting for them. The first doctor looked at each of them. He checked Lena's skin and hair. "What is your name?" he asked Lena in Italian.

"Lena Martini," she answered in a loud, clear voice. The doctor nodded.

The second doctor scared Lena. He held a long metal hook in one hand. As Lena came up to him, he slipped the hook under her eyelid and flipped it back. It hurt! Lena bit her lip to keep from yelling. The doctor just nodded and motioned her to keep going.

A young man walking behind the Martinis was not so lucky. The doctor looked at the man's eyes. He just shook his head. Then he took a piece of chalk and marked the letters *CT* on the man's coat. He pulled the young man out of line and told him to go into another room.

Lena saw other immigrants going into that room. Each one had a chalk mark on his or her coat. She wondered what those letters meant. No one in her family received one.

The Martinis all passed the medical exam. Then they walked into a huge room. A row of desks lined the front of the room. The rest of the room was divided into sections by metal pipes topped with mesh fencing.

A man motioned the Martinis to sit in one of the sections. Lena looked up at the fence and shook her head. "I feel like an animal in a cage," she said to Mary.

Nick stopped a moment to talk to the man. Then he hurried over to join his family. "We have to listen for our identification numbers to be called," he said. He held up the numbered tag he was given at the steamship office back in Genoa. "Then we have to go up to the desk and answer questions."

"More questions!"
Lena's mother said
with a sigh. "I
thought we could just
get off the ship and
go into New York."

"More questions!" Lena's mother said with a sigh. "I thought we could just get off the ship and go into New York."

The Martinis waited a long time for their numbers to be called. "I'm thirsty," Mary whined. Lena was thirsty too. But there was nothing she could do about it. Then she saw a young woman walking through the crowd. The woman held a pitcher and a cup.

"Hello," she said to the Martinis in Italian. "Would you like some water?"

"Yes, please," Lena's mother said. "My children are very thirsty and tired. Do you work here?"

"I work for the Italian Welfare League," the woman said. She handed Lena a cup of water. "We help immigrants from Italy. Do you need a place to stay or help finding a relative? Someone from our organization will help you."

"Our papa is supposed to meet us here," Lena told the woman. "But I don't know how we will ever find him."

"There is a meeting place outside this room," the woman told her. "Does your papa know what ship you sailed on?"

"Yes," Lena's mother said. "We sent him a letter before we left Italy."

32

"Then he knows that you will be here today. He is probably waiting for you outside. But if he isn't, just let me know. The Italian Welfare League will find him!"

After several hours, Lena finally heard her number called. Along with her mother, brother, and sister, she made her way to the front of the room. Two men waited for them at a desk. One man held a familiar piece of paper. Lena recognized the form. It was the one the man at the steamship office had filled out when he gave the Martinis their numbers.

The man with the paper spoke to the family in English. The man next to him translated his words into Italian. They asked the Martinis many questions.

What a nosy man! Lena thought. He wanted to know their names, ages, and where they were born. Then he asked what type of work Nick and Mama could do. He also wanted to know if they had any family in America already.

The questions weren't that hard. But Lena knew it was important to answer them right. The man scared her. Would he send them back to Italy if they gave the wrong answer? While they were waiting for their turn, she had seen several people taken into another room. What had happened to them?

Fortunately, the man seemed to like the answers the Martini family gave him. He nodded and gave them a piece of paper. The **interpreter** said it was a **landing card**. This card gave the Martinis permission to enter America.

Lena felt like cheering! Finally, the family could leave this crowded, scary place. They could look for Papa and Uncle Mario. Then she looked around at all the people and shivered. How would they ever find Papa in such a crowd?

Everyone who had passed the inspection moved to the other side of the room. Lena saw a group of people standing on the opposite side of a partition that divided the room. Suddenly, her mother began to wave. Lena saw a man waving back. It was Papa!

Lena and Mary ran forward into Papa's arms. They had not seen him for two years. But they recognized him right away. Mama was right behind them. Papa gave her a big kiss, right in front of everybody! Then he clapped Nick on the back and grabbed him tight around the shoulders.

"My family is together again at last," Papa said happily.

"Where is Uncle Mario?" Nick asked.

"He is at work," Papa said. "I took the day off to meet you."

Papa led the family through the crowd toward a flight of stairs. "We will catch a ferry to New York City," he said. "Then we will go to our apartment. It is very different from our house in Italy. But I think you will like it."

The family hurried down a flight of stairs. At the bottom, the family turned left toward a door marked

"Push to New York." Just then, Lena saw her friend Theresa.

"Wait, Papa, please," Lena said. "I have to see my friend."

Lena ran over to Theresa. She and her parents were walking to the right.

"We are going to buy tickets at the railroad station," Theresa explained. "Then we are going to Pennsylvania. My aunt and uncle live there. We are going to live with them."

"What is that?" Lena asked. She pointed to the box Theresa was holding.

Theresa opened the box. Inside was an apple, a piece of pie, and some meat between sliced bread. "The Americans call this a *sandwich*," Theresa said, pointing to the meat and bread. "I never heard of such a thing. But it looks good! I bought this for $1 from a stand over there. I'll eat it on the train."

Lena hugged her friend and wished her luck. Then she ran back to join her own family. It was time to enter New York City . . . her new home.

# CHAPTER 6

# Exams, Hearings, and Help

Why did doctors make chalk marks on people's clothing? Why were some people taken to other rooms? Who were the strangers who were so willing to help the immigrants?

These were just a few of the questions Lena had while on Ellis Island. Many of the procedures were not just for the good of the immigrants. They also benefited the U.S. citizens.

## The Medical Exam

Most immigrants who came to the eastern United States passed through Ellis Island. And each one had to have a medical exam. This was to make sure the immigrants were healthy and able to work. The exams also made sure that people with **contagious** diseases would not enter the U.S. and make other people sick.

One of the most contagious diseases in those days was

## Letter Identification

These symbols were used to mark immigrants who had medical problems.

| | |
|---|---|
| B—back | CT—trachoma |
| F—face | SC—scalp |
| K—hernia | N—neck |
| PG—pregnancy | H—heart disease |
| C—**conjunctivitis** | E—eyes |
| FT—feet | X—mental illness |
| L—lameness | P—lungs |
| S—**senility** | G—**goiter** |

**trachoma.** Trachoma was a serious eye infection that caused blindness. The doctors at Ellis Island looked for trachoma with a metal buttonhook. The buttonhook lifted the immigrant's eyelid. Then the doctors were able to look under the lid for signs of the disease.

The buttonhook was dipped in a dish of alcohol between immigrants to clean it. Anyone who had trachoma was sent home immediately.

If either doctor thought a person was sick, he marked

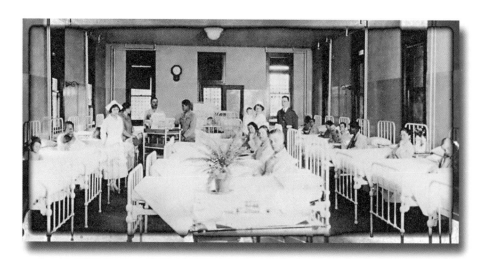

letters on the immigrant's coat with chalk. These immigrants were pulled out of line. They were then taken to a private room for a more complete exam.

Some immigrants had medical conditions that could be cured. They were sent to a hospital on the island until they were better. But some immigrants had diseases or conditions that could not be cured. They were sent back home on the next ship. Sometimes families were torn apart because one member was too sick to be admitted into the U.S.

## The Board of Special Inquiry

About ten percent of immigrants were held for legal hearings. They had to appear before a **Board of Special Inquiry**. These hearings decided if immigrants should be allowed to enter the U.S.

Some immigrants were considered unable to work and support themselves because of illnesses or a lack of skills. Some were suspected of being criminals. These people were given yellow cards marked *S.I.* (Special Inquiry).

Three Boards of Special Inquiry were usually in session all day. And a fourth was sometimes added during busy periods. Each board held 50 to 100 hearings a day. An interpreter was also present.

Each board listened to an immigrant's reasons why he or she should be allowed to enter the U.S. Friends and relatives were also allowed to speak.

Sometimes the board decided an immigrant would not be admitted to the country. That person could then appeal to the government in Washington, D.C.

**Immigrant-aid societies** often provided lawyers to handle these appeals. The immigrant had to wait on Ellis Island until the final decision was made. This usually took several weeks. Only about two percent of those who appeared before the boards were finally denied permission to enter.

*Ellis Island Welfare Library*

## Immigrant-Aid Societies

When immigrants arrived, they faced a new language, different customs, and a whole new way of life. Many immigrants received help from immigrant-aid societies.

Many groups worked at Ellis Island and the other major ports of entry. They made sure that immigrants were treated well and had everything they needed to make a good start in America.

Some groups were religious organizations. For example, the Hebrew Sheltering and Immigrant-Aid Society aided Jews.

There were groups to help almost every nationality. These included the Scandinavian-American Society and the Italian Welfare League. They helped immigrants from a specific part of the world.

Other organizations were the Red Cross, YMCA, Salvation Army, and the Travelers' Aid Society. They helped all immigrants no matter where they were from.

Aid societies provided food and water to immigrants waiting at Ellis Island. They could also arrange legal help for those who were not allowed to enter the U.S. Aid societies sent telegrams and helped find family members already in America. They arranged transportation within the U.S. They provided housing and even found jobs. These societies made a real difference in the lives of hundreds of thousands of immigrants.

# Home in America

The ferry ride to New York City was very short. When they got off, Papa led the family across a busy street. "We're going to ride the **trolley**," he said. "It's a streetcar that runs on tracks. It gets its power from an overhead electrical wire."

Lena held tight to Papa's hand as they walked to the trolley stop. The family waited with a crowd of people.

Suddenly, a car appeared on the track in front of them.

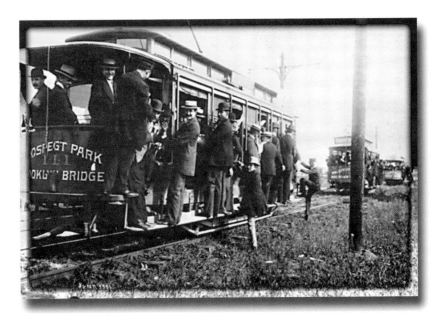

It looked like a railroad car. It had a long pole that stretched to the wire above the track. Everyone crowded on.

Lena held her breath as the car pulled away. The car rocked from side to side. It reminded her of the rolling ship at sea.

The trolley made several stops. Finally, Papa said it was time to get off. The Martinis walked slowly down the street.

Lena could hardly believe her eyes. Buildings crowded close together. They ran up one side of the street and down the other. Lines of clothes hung from the windows, drying in the breeze. Somewhere, a man with a big voice sang in Italian. The street was full of people, all speaking Italian. The air was full of the smell of Italian cooking.

"Welcome to **Little Italy**," Papa said. "Everyone who lives in this

"Welcome to Little Italy," Papa said. "Everyone who lives in this neighborhood is from Italy. This is our new home."

neighborhood is from Italy. This is our new home."

The family followed Papa into one of the buildings. Then they climbed three flights of stairs.

"This is our apartment," Papa said. He unlocked the door and stepped aside so they could enter.

Lena and Mary quickly ran through the apartment. They looked at everything. The apartment was small but very neat. The kitchen held a stove, a sink, a table and chairs, and a few shelves.

Papa turned on the faucet and let the water run for a minute. "Cold water," he said. "This apartment is called a **cold-water flat.**"

The apartment also had a bedroom. "We will all sleep in this room," Papa said. Lena knew that would be crowded. But she didn't mind.

"Where is the bathroom?" Mary asked.

"The bathroom is down the hall," Papa said. "Everyone on the floor has to share it."

Lena remembered the outhouse they had on the farm in Italy. She hated going outside to use the bathroom, especially at night. Having a bathroom right down the hall would be wonderful!

"*Buon giorno*! Hello!" a familiar voice called.

Lena squealed with delight. She ran for the front door.

"Uncle Mario!" she called.

Her uncle swept Lena up in a big hug. His clothes were dusty. And his hands were gray with dirt. But Lena didn't care. She was thrilled to see him.

That night, the family ate dinner together for the first time in two years. Mama cooked pasta with a thick tomato sauce. Lena chopped vegetables fresh from the market down the street. Then they sat around the table and talked late into the night.

"Uncle Mario and I have good jobs," Papa said. "We are **bricklayers**. There are so many new buildings going up. New homes and factories are built every day. Many of the workers are Italian. We finish putting up one building. Then we start building another one."

"Can I get a job laying bricks?" Nick asked.

"Yes," Papa said. "I already told my boss about you. You will come to work with me tomorrow. And I will teach you how to make these big, strong buildings."

"Do I have to go to work too?" Lena asked. "And what about Mary?"

"Mary is too little to work," Papa said. "She will stay home with Mama at first. When she is five years old, she can go to school. You can go to school now, Lena."

"How can we pay to send two girls to school?" Mama wondered.

"School is free here," Papa told her. "Anyone can go. We don't have to pay anything. In fact, there is a law in America. It says children must go to school until they are 16."

> "School is free here," Papa told her. "Anyone can go."

Mama smiled. "Education is very important," she said. "You girls will learn to read, write, and speak English. Then you will teach me and your papa. We will make a good life here."

Lena started school the very next day. Her mother took her to the school office. No one in the office spoke Italian. But many of the students did. The principal called on one of the older students to translate for them.

Lena told the principal her name and that she was 12 years old. She told him that she had gone to school in Italy and could read in Italian. The principal told the older student to take Lena to the classroom where the other 12-year-olds were.

"You will learn English from the other students," he said.

Lena kissed her mother good-bye. Then she followed the student to her new classroom. The teacher introduced her to the other children. Lena smiled nervously at the curious faces staring back at her. The class was very large and crowded. There weren't even enough desks for everyone. Lena had to share a desk with a girl named Lucy.

Lucy didn't seem very happy to share her desk. "I suppose you don't speak English," she said with a sniff. Lena shook her head.

"You'd better learn," Lucy said. Then she sat as far away from Lena as she could. "Italians are dirty," she said. "I hope I don't catch any bugs from your clothes or your hair."

"Be quiet, Lucy," said a boy sitting behind them. He smiled at Lena. "My name is Carlo," he said in Italian. "Lucy doesn't like Italians. Many people here don't. But I will help you."

"Carlo, speak in English, please," said the teacher. "We don't speak Italian in this classroom. We're in America now."

Lena bowed her head and stared at her books. She tried not to cry. Words flowed over her as the students recited their lessons. She didn't understand any of them. The only subject that made sense to her was math. At least numbers were the same in any language!

As the days passed, school became easier for Lena. Carlo turned out to be a good friend. He introduced Lena to the other Italian students in the class. They sat together at lunch and shared their food. And they played together outside. Sometimes the American children played with them. But usually the two groups stayed apart.

"I suppose you don't speak English," she said with a sniff. Lena shook her head.

Soon Lena found herself learning English. At first, it was just a few words here and there. Then she began to understand the stories in her reader.

Carlo had been in America for a year. He already spoke English very well. He was a big help to Lena.

When Lena came home from school, her mother and father were at work. Mama had found a job in a factory. She made dresses. She worked from early morning until six o'clock at night. A neighbor down the hall watched Mary while everyone worked. Lena took care of Mary when she came home from school.

Every night, as the family ate dinner, Mama and Papa asked Lena what new English words she had learned. She carefully printed the words on a piece of paper so the rest of the family could learn them.

Papa always brought home an Italian newspaper. One day, he brought home an American paper called *The World*.

Together, he and Lena read the stories.

"I am learning English too," Papa said proudly.

"I know another way you can learn English," Uncle Mario said. "Someone at work told me about a place called a **settlement house**. It has classes there for adults to learn English and other things. They also have programs for children."

"How much do these things cost?" Mama asked suspiciously.

"They are free," Uncle Mario said. "Everyone who works there is a volunteer. I would like to go to this settlement house and see what they do."

So after supper the next evening, the whole family went to visit the settlement house. Lena couldn't believe her eyes. There was so much going on! Some rooms were filled with adults sitting at desks. They were reciting words in English. Lena giggled. She had never heard of grown-ups going to school!

"Those people are taking a **citizenship** class," explained a worker named Annie. "They are learning all about the U.S. and our government. Then they will take a test. If they pass the test and show they can be good Americans, they will become citizens.

That means they can live in this country for the rest of their lives. They will enjoy the same rights as someone who was born here."

Another room was filled with machines. Boys Nick's age were cutting wood and building things. "These boys are learning a trade," said Annie. "After they learn woodworking, they will be able to get a job. We teach many other trades here too."

In another room, a group of children were singing and playing instruments. Lena recognized a song she had heard in Italy.

Annie smiled at Lena. "Maybe you would like to join our children's orchestra," she said. "They give concerts for the people in the community."

"These boys are learning a trade," said Annie. "After they learn wood-working, they will be able to get a job. We teach many other trades here too."

Then Annie took the Martinis to a room filled with toys. Little Mary's eyes lit up with excitement. Annie turned to Mama. "Many children spend the day here while their parents are working," she said. "We have lots of toys and games. And there is a playground outside. We also teach the children English. Mary is welcome to join us."

"Our neighbor watches Mary while we work. But she doesn't take very good care of her," Mama said. "One time Lena came home and found Mary playing in the street. No one was watching her!"

"That won't happen here," Annie said. "We have three teachers watching the children. They take very good care of them."

Mary pulled at Mama's long skirt. "Can I come here, Mama? Please?"

Mama smiled. "We will try it. Maybe Papa and I will even come here to study. There is so much to do here!"

Lena, Mary, Nick, Papa, and Uncle Mario enjoyed the activities at the settlement house. But Mama often had to stay home and work. The family needed money. Mama's job at the dress factory did not pay very much. She often brought material home to sew and make extra money. This work was called *piecework*. Mama was paid a few cents for every piece she made.

Lena felt bad seeing her mother working so hard. "I will quit school and go to work too," she said one night.

"No, Lena," Mama said firmly. "You are too young to quit school. The **truant officer** will come. Then we will get into trouble. You must stay in school until you are 16. Then you can go to work."

"But I want to help you!" Lena said.

"I have an idea," Mama said. "You can do piecework too. Many women at the factory bring work home for their children."

"I have an idea," Mama said. "You can do piecework too. Many women at the factory bring work home for their children."

Lena quickly agreed. She already knew how to sew. And she wanted to help her family.

So every day after school, Lena sat in the kitchen of the apartment and sewed dresses. Almost every night, her mother came home with more piecework for her to do.

After she helped her mother cook supper, Lena quickly did her

50

homework. Then she went back to work. She was proud to be earning money for her family. Even Mary helped sometimes.

Lena worked hard at school and at home. But she had fun too. Many Italian children lived in the neighborhood. And more arrived every day. The children enjoyed playing in the street and on the playground of the settlement house. Sometimes, if they had a nickel to pay the trolley fare, the children would go to the zoo in Central Park.

Two years after Lena arrived in America, Uncle Mario sat down to supper. He had a smile on his face. He had big news. He was getting married to an Italian woman. She worked in the market. The Martini family was very happy.

"Are you going to live here after you and Concetta get married?" Lena asked.

Uncle Mario looked serious. "I don't know. It is very crowded in this apartment already. This whole city is very crowded! I miss living in the country. Remember how beautiful it was on the farm in Italy?"

Lena's father cleared his throat. "I have something to say," he said. "You know I save some money out of every paycheck. We have been together in this country for two years now. I have saved enough money to buy a little farm in the country. It is close enough that Mario, Nick, and I can still take the train to work here in the city. But it is far enough away that we can have enough room to grow our own food and raise some cows and chickens. Mario, if you and Concetta would like to join us, we could all live on the farm together. It will be just like in the old days in Italy."

Lena's mother smiled. "It would be nice to live in the country again," she said.

"I would rather work on a farm than in the city," Nick added.

The family talked late into the night. Finally, they

decided to leave New York City and buy the little farm about 30 miles away.

When Lena went to bed that night, she couldn't sleep. Part of her was happy to leave New York City and live in the country again. Mama even said she could have a dog or a cat for a pet!

But part of her liked it here. She had many friends at school and in the neighborhood. There was always something fun to do. It would be hard to start a new life.

"We can do it," Lena said. "After all, we came all the way to America from Italy. We crossed a huge ocean. We learned a new language. We left our old life behind and started over in America."

Lena pulled the covers up to her chin. Back in Italy, Uncle Mario had said that the streets in America were paved with gold. That was not true. The streets were made of dirt and stone, just like they were in Italy. But America was a golden land of **opportunity**. Lena knew her family would have to work hard and help one another. Then they would succeed. They would have a good life no matter where they lived.

Lena was glad to be in America!

# Settlement Houses and Citizenship

## Settlement Houses

Settlement houses were like today's community centers. They were usually found in the poor neighborhoods of large cities. Their goal was to help immigrants improve their lives and become **Americanized.**

The very first settlement house was Toynbee Hall. It was founded in London, England, in 1884. Two ministers "settled" in a house in a poor neighborhood. They wanted to study the people who lived there. The two men believed they could only understand the poor and their problems if they lived among them. The ministers invited other people to join them. Soon Toynbee Hall was providing services to the people of the neighborhood.

The settlement movement quickly spread to the U.S. In 1886, a man named Stanton Coit opened the first U.S. settlement house. It was on the Lower East Side of New York. He called his house the Neighborhood Guild. By

1900, there were 100 settlement houses across the nation.

The most famous member of the movement was Jane Addams. In 1889, she and a friend named Ellen Gates founded Hull House in Chicago, Illinois. Hull House's mission was to "provide a center for a higher civic and social life" and to "investigate and improve the conditions in the industrial districts of Chicago."

Addams and other workers lived at Hull House. They provided services to as many as 2,000 Greek, Italian, Russian, and German immigrants. These services included citizenship and English classes, child care, health and hygiene classes, hot meals, and job training.

Settlement houses did more than provide services to residents of poor neighborhoods. They also pushed for **social reform**.

Jane Addams and her volunteers worked for laws to protect workers and children. They led the fight for an eight-hour workday and a six-day workweek. They pushed for no labor for anyone under 16 and accident and unemployment insurance.

Other settlement houses worked to build public playgrounds, swimming pools, and theaters. These would improve the quality of life for neighborhood residents, especially children.

## Citizenship and Naturalization

To enjoy all the benefits of living in America, immigrants had to become citizens. But not all became citizens. Others became citizens only after they had lived here for many years.

Immigrants who lived in the U.S. without becoming citizens were called **aliens**. Those who chose to become citizens went through a process called *naturalization*.

In 1906, the U.S. government passed the **Naturalization Act**. This law created a three-step procedure to gain citizenship. This basic procedure is still used today.

After 1906, an immigrant began the process of citizenship by filing "first papers." These indicated a desire to become naturalized. Next the immigrant filed "second papers." These papers formally requested citizenship.

During the next three months, the government investigated the immigrant's background. If he or she had been involved in criminal activities, citizenship was denied. Two witnesses had to swear that the person had good moral character. Finally, he or she had to answer questions about American history and politics. And the immigrant had to speak some English. When all these requirements had been met, the person became a U.S. citizen.

After World War I (1914–1918), many people in the U.S. did not trust foreigners. There was a lot of anti-immigrant feelings. This was especially true for those who had dark skin or who just "looked different."

Because of these feelings, stricter laws were passed. These laws limited immigration and citizenship. Perhaps the

hardest-hit group were the Chinese. They weren't allowed to become naturalized until 1943.

In 1952, the U.S. government passed the **McCarran-Walter Act**. This law ended all racial restrictions on naturalization. It also ended restrictions based on sex and marital status. The law stated that citizens had to be able to read, write, and speak English. Aliens were required to register with the government each year. This made it easier to **deport**, or return, aliens to their homelands, if needed.

Since the McCarran-Walter Act was passed, immigration to the U.S. has reached record levels. So has the number of naturalized citizens. In 1996, about 1.6 million resident aliens applied for citizenship. By 1997, the U.S. had more than 9 million naturalized citizens out of a foreign-born population of almost 26 million.

# CHAPTER 9

# What Immigrants Gave to America

Lena Martini and her family helped change America.

The people of the U.S. represent many countries. Settlers came from England, Spain, France, and other European countries in the 17th and 18th centuries. Millions of Africans were brought by force as slaves. Europeans and Asians flooded the U.S. between 1850 and 1922. They were part of the biggest wave of immigrants in history.

*San Francisco's Chinatown in about 1900*

## Famous Immigrants

| Name | Homeland | Year | Career |
|------|----------|------|--------|
| Irving Berlin (1888–1989) | Russia | 1892 | songwriter |
| Knute Rockne (1888–1931) | Norway | 1893 | football coach |
| Felix Frankfurter (1882–1965) | Austria | 1894 | Supreme Court justice |
| Samuel Goldwyn (1881–1974) | Poland | 1896 | film industry mogul |
| Pauline Newman (1894–1986) | Lithuania | 1901 | labor leader |
| Frank Capra (1897–1991) | Italy | 1903 | movie director |
| Bob Hope (1903–  ) | England | 1908 | comedian |
| Bela Lugosi (1882–1956) | Hungary | 1921 | actor |
| Isaac Asimov (1920–1992) | Russia | 1923 | scientist–author |
| Henry Kissinger (1923–  ) | Germany | 1938 | statesman |
| Werner VonBraun (1912–1977) | Germany | 1945 | rocket scientist |
| Mikhail Baryshnikov (1948–  ) | Russia | 1974 | dancer |
| Gloria Estefan (1957–  ) | Cuba | 1959 | singer |

Today, new arrivals come from Central America, China, Vietnam, Haiti, and many other countries. They continue to change the face of our nation.

Millions of immigrants have made America their home. Therefore, we live in a **multicultural** society. Almost every day, we are exposed to something that has come from another country.

One of the most interesting influences in our lives is food. Many foods that we enjoy today were brought here from somewhere else. Noodles were invented in China thousands of years ago. A form of pizza came from Italy. Burritos, tacos, and fajitas were brought by Hispanic immigrants from Central America. Sushi is raw fish and rice wrapped in seaweed. It is a favorite food in Japan. All of these foods are popular in America today.

Our holidays also reflect our immigrant roots. Christmas was first celebrated in Europe. Hanukkah and Rosh Hashanah are part of the Jewish culture. Kwanzaa celebrates principles in the African tradition. And many Americans of all cultures enjoy ethnic holidays such as Chinese New Year, St. Patrick's Day, and Cinco de Mayo.

Immigrants also built America. Like Lena's papa and uncle, many Italians worked in the construction industry. New York City's tall buildings could not have been built without their labor.

The same thing is true of cities all over America. And many of the farmers who fed our country during the late 1800s and early 1900s came from Ireland, Sweden, Germany, and England. They, too, helped make America the most powerful nation in the world.

America used to be called a *melting pot*. It was thought that immigrants would leave their traditions behind and "melt" into American culture.

But more recently, America has been called a stew. Each ethnic group retains its own flavor. But all these flavors blend together to create a wonderful meal unlike anything else. The strength of America is found in its many different peoples. And they came from all over the world—to become Americans.

# GLOSSARY

alien — immigrant who lives in a country without becoming a citizen

Americanized — acquired American characteristics

antiseptic — substance that kills germs and prevents infection

Board of Special Inquiry — group of officials who decided if an immigrant should be allowed to enter the U.S.

bricklayer — person who lays bricks to create walls, buildings, or other structures

cholera — deadly disease that causes severe diarrhea

citizenship — rights, privileges, and duties that come with being a member of a particular country

cold-water flat — apartment that has only cold running water

Communist — person who follows a political system where all the land and buildings belong to the government

conjunctivitis — inflammation of the eye

contagious — spread by direct contact

deport — to send people back to their own country

Ellis Island — government inspection station near New York City that examined millions of immigrants between 1892–1954

ethnic group

people sharing the same national origin, language, or culture

famine

widespread lack of food

ferry

small ship that carries people and vehicles across a short stretch of water

fumigate

to apply chemicals to destroy pests

goiter

swelling of the front of the neck that indicates an enlarged thyroid gland

homeland

person's native country; place where a person was born

Homestead Act

law passed by the U.S. government in the 1860s that gave free land to anyone who lived on it for five years

immigrant-aid society

group who helped immigrants. Services often included providing food and water, arranging legal help, sending telegrams, helping find families, arranging transportation, securing housing, and finding jobs.

immigration

act of coming from one country to live in another

industrialization

growth in businesses and factories due to advances in machinery

interpreter

person who translates one language to another language

landing card

card given to immigrants giving them permission to enter America

lice

plural of *louse*; small insect that lives on plants or warm-blooded animals and sucks the blood and juices

| | |
|---|---|
| Little Italy | neighborhood with many Italian immigrants |
| McCarran-Walter Act | law passed in 1952 that changed American immigration policy |
| multicultural | representing many different cultures or ethnic groups |
| naturalization | process of becoming a citizen of a country |
| Naturalization Act | law passed in 1906 that created a three-step procedure to gain American citizenship |
| opportunity | chance to do something |
| peasant | person who works on a farm, especially in Europe and Asia |
| persecution | being treated unfairly because of their political or religious beliefs |
| piecework | work done by the piece and paid for by a set rate for each piece |
| pogrom | organized killing of a specific group of people |
| refugee | person who is forced to leave home because of war, persecution, or natural disaster |
| Refugee Acts | special laws passed by the U.S. during the 1950s to admit Eastern European immigrants fleeing Communist governments |
| seaport | city or town with a harbor where ships can dock |